WILD and
SWAMPY

WILD and SWAMPY

EXPLORING WITH
JIM ARNOSKY

HarperCollins*Publishers*

Acrylics were used for the full-color illustrations. The sketches were done in pen-and-ink. The text type is 14-point Caxton.

Wild and Swampy
Copyright © 2000 by Jim Arnosky

Printed in Singapore at Tien Wah Press.

www.harperchildrens.com

Library of Congress Cataloging-in-Publication Data
Arnosky, Jim.
Wild and swampy / exploring with Jim Arnosky.
p. cm.
Summary: Describes and portrays the birds, snakes, and other animals that can be seen in a swamp.
ISBN 0-688-17119-2 (trade) — ISBN 0-688-17120-6 (library)
1. Swamp animals—Pictorial Works—Juvenile literature.   [1. Swamp animals.]   I. Title.
QL114.5A75 2000   591.768—dc21   99-52381

3 4 5 6 7 8 9 10
❖

Louisiana bayou

For Tony and Barbara

Okefenokee Swamp

Great blue heron

Green heron

Introduction

A swamp is a wetland with trees and shrubs growing up out of the water. There are hardwood swamps thickly grown with red maples, ash, alders, or willows. There are bogs and swamps where cedar, fur, spruce, tamarack, or cypress trees thrive. In tropical areas there are coastal swamps where red mangrove trees stand in salty water.

Swamps are incredibly beautiful places. Water and trees, sun and shadows, green leaves and hanging moss combine to make spectacular scenes. But to see these things safely, a person must stay up out of the water, either by sitting in a stable boat, standing on a sturdy boardwalk, or riding in a car on a raised road.

Hardwood swamp

Bayou scene

*Alligator resting—
Okefenokee Swamp*

Each spring my wife Deanna and I leave the snow-covered hills of Vermont and travel south to places where the water is warm and the land is wild and swampy. The paintings in this book are of some of the swamp creatures we have seen. The journal-style pen-and-ink sketches depict different swamps. Turn the pages and explore them with me.

—Jim Arnosky
Ramtails 2000

Mangrove swamp

Sheltered from the wind by tree trunks, branches, and leaves, the water in a swamp can be as still as glass. Stained from black rotting vegetation and by the reddish-brown tannic acid leaching out of tree bark, swamp water is dark and highly reflective. Every swamp scene is really two scenes—one upright, one upside-down.

The stillness in a swamp can actually help you locate wildlife. Any disturbance in the water is most likely being made by an animal.

Bald cypress swamp

A ripple in the still water alerted me to this egret's presence. The first part of the bird I noticed was its white tail feathers sticking out from behind a cypress tree. Then, on the opposite side of the tree, I spotted the bird's outstretched neck. A long leg and slowly stepping foot, a momentary flash of wing, the yellow bill poking forward—this is how I saw the egret as it silently stalked the shallow water for fish.

I always feel a mixture of excitement and caution when I'm in a swamp—especially a southern swamp. The animals that are abundantly found in the warm South are those I see least often in my cool northern hills. I'm talking about snakes—nonvenomous and venomous, small and large. This southern brown water snake was five feet long and as thick as my upper arm. That's a great big water snake!

The nonvenomous brown water snake is the snake most often mistaken for a venomous cottonmouth moccasin. It's easy to see why. The two snakes are found in the same places. They have similar markings, and both have triangular heads.

Water snake on a limb

This is a cottonmouth moccasin! Those of you who live where these venomous snakes live know how dangerous they can be. Even though I was safe, up on a boardwalk looking down at this snake, I could feel the hair on the back of my neck stiffen. Look at the sharply triangular head. See how the snake's coloration blends perfectly with that of the ground.

The color of cottonmouths varies from place to place. I have seen moccasins that were light brown with distinctive markings, and others that were completely black. In some parts of their range, cottonmouths are muddy brown. The cottonmouth moccasin is named for the pinkish white lining inside its mouth, which it sometimes displays as a warning before it finally strikes.

Cottonmouth moccasin displaying mouth

We saw the water snake and the cottonmouth in a cypress swamp where thousand-year-old trees, some twenty feet in circumference, stand one hundred feet tall. Fallen cypress trunks lie across the water. And growing up throughout the swamp are hundreds of smoothly rounded tree stubs called cypress knees. There is more shade than sunlight in a cypress swamp. Daytime looks more like dusk, dusk like night. Nocturnal creatures such as the yellow-crowned night heron are active all day long. This night heron was the first I have ever been able to see so clearly and vividly.

Yellow rat snake

In the cypress swamp Deanna and I followed a narrow boardwalk that led us deeper and deeper into the silence. The only sounds we heard were our own footsteps on the wooden planks. Then, somewhere in the distance, a barred owl called, *"Who-hoo-hoo-hoooooo."* All around us we saw only trees and water until another barred owl, perched right above us in a tupelo-gum tree, hooted back, *"Who-hoo-hoo-hoooooo."* Barred owls are found in many swamps. Their call, which sounds like someone asking, "Who cooks for you?" is a familiar swamp sound. This owl called again, then spread its wings and flew noiselessly to another perch. When most owls are sleeping, these swamp-dwelling owls are wide-awake, hunting all day long. When do they sleep?

Swamp boardwalk

Where I live, raccoons are night creatures. But in the southern swamplands, raccoons hunt during the day, when they are less likely to bump into a hungry alligator. Alligators normally feed after dark.

One day in Georgia, in Okefenokee Swamp, I saw a raccoon wading in a canal. At one point the raccoon waded right by a large alligator half-hidden on the grassy bank. The alligator immediately began crawling toward the raccoon. Unaware that it was being stalked, the raccoon stopped to fish in the water with its front paws. The alligator froze in its muddy tracks. The raccoon began to wade again. The alligator followed, inching closer and closer. When it was within striking distance of the raccoon, the alligator sank itself deeper into the greenery, getting ready to rush forward. Some dry grass rustled. The raccoon heard and scurried away.

Great blue heron

Raccoons, opossums, otters, bobcats, black bear, and deer all thrive in swampland. But seeing these mammals, in a swamp, is much more difficult than seeing the reptiles and birds. Mammals do not sun themselves in the open the way reptiles do. Nor do they draw attention to themselves by sudden movements or loud sounds the way birds do. Every mammal sighting in a swamp is a surprise.

To keep their fur from becoming waterlogged, swamp-dwelling mammals must make use of every little bit of higher ground. Even a clump of matted grass can be a dry island for a wet and weary swamp mammal.

Imagine we are in a boat gliding on a narrow waterway. Long strands of Spanish moss hanging from low tree limbs block our view of the mud bank. The little boat reaches an opening between drooping moss, and you spot an alligator. Its mouth hangs open in what looks like a comical smile, resting and relaxing the all-important jaw muscles. The alligator tracks us with its eyes as we slowly drift away, following the lazy flow of water through the bayou.

A bayou is a swamp that leads to a larger body of water such as a river, lake, or even the salty sea. Some bayous are not very swampy at all. The saltwater channels and lagoons in tropical mangrove swamps are bayous connected to the sea.

Mangrove swamps are named for the mangrove trees that stand up out of the water, supported by strong arched roots. The exposed roots create a water-level wildlife habitat that rivals the habitat provided by the mangroves' leafy branches.

This painting shows an anhinga, or snake bird, swimming underwater between and around the mangrove roots, spearfishing with its long sharp bill. After fishing, the water-soaked bird perches on the mangrove treetop to spread its wings and dry out.

Seeking refuge from predators, mangrove crabs climb from their saltwater habitat up the mangrove trees to branches as high as twenty feet. Crabs up in the trees, birds down underwater—that's a mangrove swamp in a nutshell!

Anhinga drying wings

Have you ever seen a pelican this closely? I have. I saw it in a mangrove swamp. Mangrove trees are just small enough so that birds perching anywhere on them can be seen and appreciated in detail.

I later saw this pelican swimming around, lunging after fish. I also watched it dive from the air and plunge for fish. Marvelous!

Sometimes I simply cannot leave a place. In the mangrove swamp I always stay until the last light, and wish the day was longer. There is so much more I want you to see—more swamps I want to show you. But we've already seen a lot, and covered miles of watery ground. Let's watch the sun go down. Soon it will be dark. Tonight you and I will dream of places wild and swampy.

Raccoon climbing mangrove roots

The pen-and-ink sketches in this book are done in exactly the same style I use in my travel journals. Carefully look at each sketch, and you will see how I quickly construct my subjects and scenes, and how I shade them. Then try to copy the style in your own journal sketches.

It's fun to sketch this way. You'll see just how lively your lines can be!

Jim Arnosky